Area and pe

Contents

Teachers' notes

Aim of this book

The aim of this book is to provide a varied and stimulating collection of activities that will supplement your existing scheme of work for mathematics. To make the most of the material it is important to read the teachers' notes which follow.

Using this book

While most of the pages in this book are intended for immediate use, many are reusable, and will last for a considerable time if covered in plastic film or kept in plastic wallets. Many of the activities in this book require the use of mathematical paper (squared or spotty) so photocopiable resource pages have been included at the back of the book so that extra paper can be made available.

The activity sheets are designed to be self-explanatory, but nonetheless each activity needs to be introduced by the teacher if the children are to make the most of it. It is also very valuable for time to be spent discussing their work after the children have finished. A reference chart for the various curriculum documents for mathematics can be found on page 4, in order to help identify where the activities fit within the programmes of study. This is often difficult to do without trying the activities, so a degree of flexibility is recommended.

Some activities could be taken home and shared with parents or other members of the family.

Mathematical content

The activities in this book encourage a very practical approach to children's understanding of area and perimeter, and the links and difference between the two. The concept of quantifying the amount of surface is a particularly difficult one for many children. Practical experience, for example measuring surfaces with hand or footprints, wrapping parcels, covering pictures with collage materials and so on, is very important. It is valuable to explore the measurement of surface in units other than squares, so that the children can see why the square has been chosen as the standard unit.

Statements relating to understanding of area and perimeter only appear at the higher levels appropriate for Key Stage 2. This leaves the earlier preparatory work undefined but nonetheless vital.

These activities have been organised in approximate order of difficulty. Examples of introductory activities are at the beginning of the book, while the last few activities are very challenging and only suitable for the most confident children.

Most of the activities in the book include opportunities for decision-making and, therefore, will encourage development of the skills and processes outlined in Attainment Target 1 (Using and applying mathematics).

Notes on individual activities

Page 5: Size order

The children should discuss with you how to set about the task, as it is not an easy one. They may, for instance, place the shapes on top of each other, ask for squared paper or a transparent squared grid. Allowing the children to choose their own approach will help you to assess their understanding of the measurement of area.

Page 6: Biscuit cutters

The children may use one cutter or a mix of two, three or four. Discussion should bring out ideas about shapes that fit together to cover a surface.

Similar activities using Plasticine or dough help reinforce the idea that surfaces can be compared or measured using non-standard units (the cutter shapes).

Page 7: Hand size

The hand shape is used as a measuring unit. Encourage the measurement of both flat and non-flat surfaces. Discuss how the children can remember what areas have already been measured and how to keep count.

Page 8: Foot size

This activity offers an introduction to quantifying area using a variety of non-standard units and should be used alongside page 7, 'Hand size'. Ask the children to explain how they compared the sizes of their hand and foot shapes.

Encourage them to realise the importance of:

- the use of a standard unit;
- choosing a standard unit that fits together to measure area (for example, cubes are better than round counters).

Page 9: How many?

The children may wish to cut out some of the shapes to compare them. This task is not as straightforward as it may at first appear.

Pages 10 and 11: How many squares? and How many triangles?

Where the measuring units are not marked on the surfaces, the areas are harder to work out. This activity encourages mental imagery of the size of the unit.

Page 12: Half a square

This is an introduction to recognising and counting half squares. If groups of children compare their work the vast number of possibilities should be appreciated. Lines can be curved too. For those who are less confident, you could suggest using squared paper underneath as a guideline. To broaden children's thinking, it often helps for them to do a few examples, share ideas and then complete the sheet.

Page 13: Counting the halves

Extension activity

Suggest choosing other sizes of shape to explore, or ask children to draw shapes for others to measure.

Use squared spotty paper to draw the shapes and measure the areas of these.

Page 14: Counting the curves

Extension activities

Draw around an irregular shape (for example, a sycamore leaf) two or three times on to squared paper. Measure the area by counting squares. Often the children's counts will not be the same, emphasising that such measurements can only be approximate.

Page 15: Making pairs

This activity, and those on pages 16–19, explore the relationship between area and perimeter. Many children find it difficult to separate the two, or to realise that, for instance, the same perimeter can enclose different areas.

Each child or group will need two copies of the 'Making pairs' page, as the shapes do not pair up in the same ways when using area and then perimeter. Displays could be mounted on coloured backing paper. Invite the children to label their work carefully, and offer explanations of what they find.

Pages 16 and 17: Arranging squares 1 and 2

At each stage this activity is greatly enhanced by discussion. You could ask the children, for instance, 'How do you know this is the smallest/largest perimeter? What other perimeters are possible? Can you suggest some that aren't possible? Are there any patterns appearing when you look at one square, two squares, three squares and so on?' The children may wish to use squared paper instead of manipulating the cut-out squares, or to draw arrangements on plain paper. Recognising the need to record their findings is an important element in Attainment Target 1 (Using and applying mathematics).

Pages 18 and 19: Perimeter possibilities 1 and 2

This is another activity that is most successfully used by groups of children rather than by individuals.

Encourage them to compare results, and check each other's work. For example, 'How many *different* shapes have we made between us?' They may assume that the diagonal across a 1cm square is also 1cm. Sometimes it is better to let them discover this for themselves, rather than be told it beforehand.

Pages 20 and 21: Rectangles 1 and 2

This activity takes some time and is probably most suitable for pairs of children. You will need to provide plenty of spare squared paper. The activity encourages understanding of the relationship between rectangles and multiplication, and thereby, how to calculate the area of squares and rectangles. The open-ended section at the end of 'Rectangles – 2', page 21, can lead to discussion of factors and prime numbers.

Remind the children that a square is also a rectangle, a special one where not only are opposite sides equal and parallel, but adjacent sides are equal too.

Page 22: How many hidden squares?

This activity offers the children the opportunity to put into practice the idea behind the activities on pages 20 and 21.

Page 23: Tangram

This sheet would be best photocopied on to card, so that the pieces of the puzzle can be used when attempting pages 24 and 25.

The emphasis here is on the relationship between the areas of the pieces.

For example: A = B   C + E = D
C + E + F = A
C = E   C + E = F

There are many more. This should help the children to appreciate better why the tangram can fit together in so many ways.

Page 24: Tangram puzzles

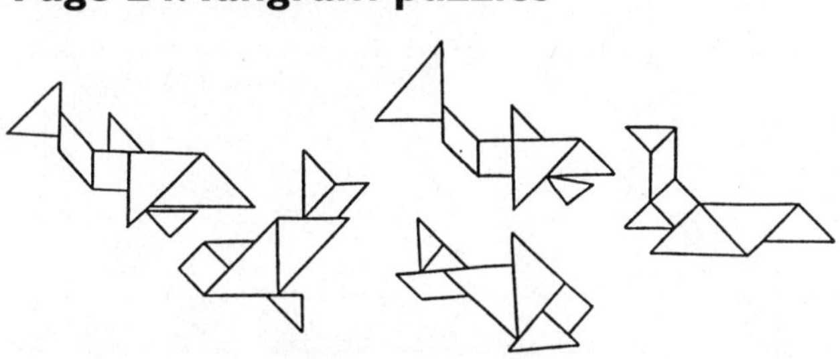

Page 25: Tangram illusions

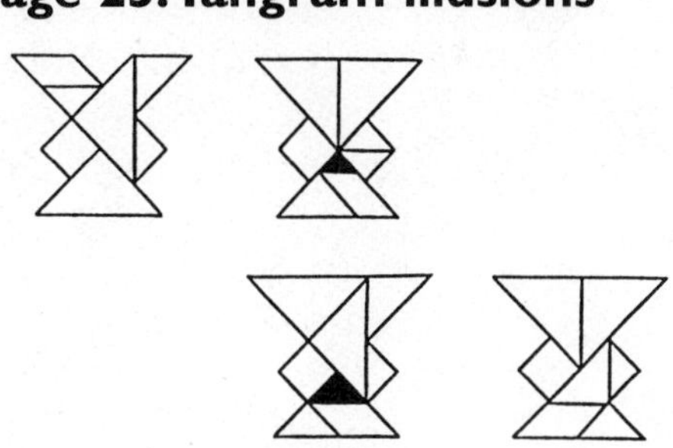

This is a very challenging activity. Allow the children to talk about what they notice before they start, for example, that the outlines are the same (or are they?). Discuss where the spaces come from. Afterwards, the children can compare results. How has the illusion been created? Discussing possibilities is more important than searching for one answer.

Pages 26 and 27: Framing miniatures 1 and 2

Plain or squared paper should be available for the children to work on, if needed. This activity would be useful for assessing problem-solving skills if they are allowed to tackle the task independently. Ask yourself (or the child):

- How did they set about the task?
- What materials/equipment/methods did they use?
- How independently could they make these decisions?
- What recording/communication skills did they use to show you what they did?
- What do they consider are the possibilities in the investigation suggested at the bottom of page 27?
- How can they be sure they have found a sensible answer?

Page 28: The farmer and his field

The nearer an area approaches a circle, the smaller the perimeter will be. The largest area will therefore be a 36-sided polygon. The absolute accuracy of this is not, however, necessary. The important thing is that children explore a variety of possibilities, showing that they understand about the way areas and perimeters can relate. Most will probably suggest a square as the best option.

A sophisticated child may suggest that the farmer should enclose a hill inside the fence, to gain more space. Of course, he or she would be right.

Pages 29–32: Photocopiable resources

These pages include 2cm and 1cm squared paper, triangular (isometric) paper and squared and triangular spotty paper to be photocopied freely as required by the children. The children's investigations can be inhibited if they are worried about fitting their work into too limited a space.

National Curriculum: Mathematics
In addition to the relevant Programme of Study for AT1, the following PoS for AT4 are relevant to the activities in the book: **Level 3** (Activities at approximately this level are included in this book, although there are no relevant PoS statements.) **Level 4** • finding perimeters of simple shapes. • finding areas by counting squares.... **Level 5** • finding areas of plane figures (excluding circles), using appropriate formulae.

Scottish 5–14 Curriculum: Mathematics

In addition to the content of the attainment outcome 'Problem solving and enquiry', the following attainment outcomes and targets are relevant to the activities in this book:

Attainment outcome	Strand	Attainment target	Level
Number, money and measurement	Measure and estimate	**Measure in standard units:** - area: shapes composed of rectangles/squares or irregular shapes using tiles or grids in square centimetres.... -	C
		Realise that... area can be conserved when shape changes;	D
		Measure in standard units: - area: right-angled triangles on cm squared grids.	
	Perimeter, Formulae, Scales	**Calculate perimeter** of simple straight-sided shapes by adding lengths.	D
		Calculate using rules: - areas of rectangles and squares.	E

◆ Name ______________________________

Size order

- Cut out the biscuits below.
- Put them in order of size, from biggest to smallest.

- Write down how you decided on your order.

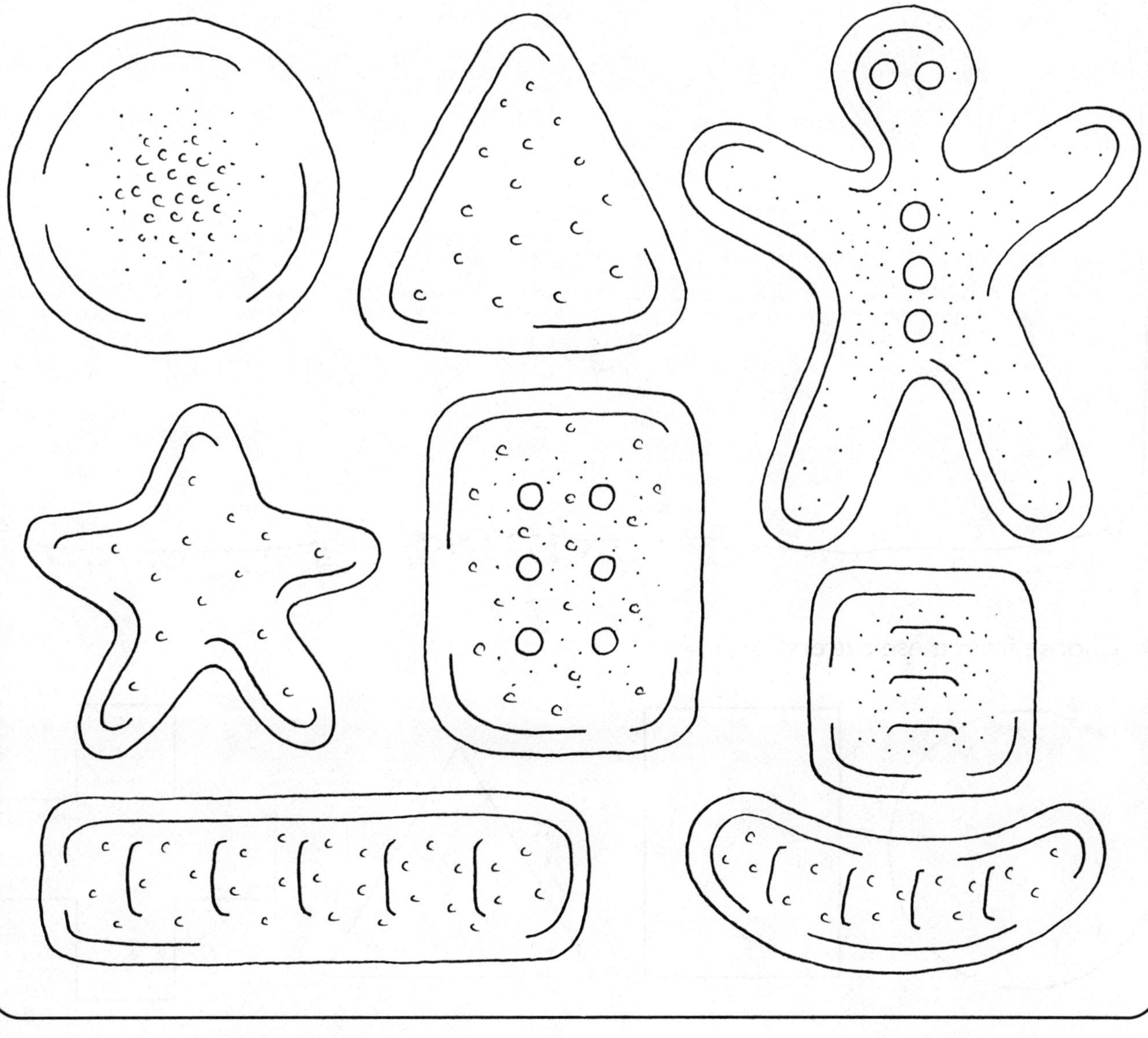

◆ Name ______________________

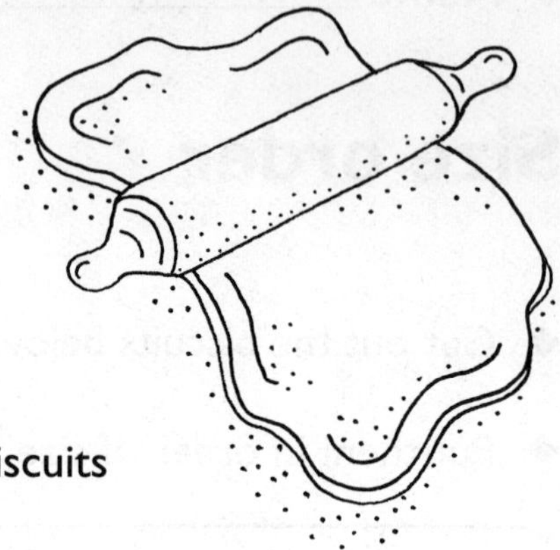

Biscuit cutters

◆ How many biscuits can you cut out of this pastry?

◆ Choose one or more cutters from the bottom of the page.
Cut them out and show by drawing how you could get as many biscuits as possible from the pastry.

◆ Choose from these cutters:

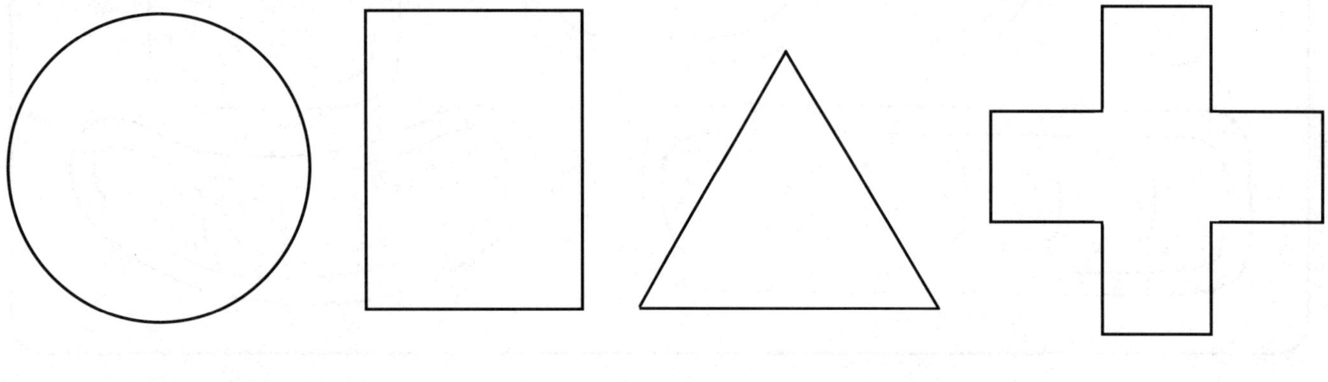

◆ Name ______________________

Hand size

◆ Draw around your hand, fingers together, in the box below.

◆ Cut out your hand shape.

◆ How many times will your hand shape fit on your chair seat? (No overlapping allowed!) ______________________

◆ Choose four surfaces to measure using hand shapes.

◆ Write your findings here:

Surface measured	Number of hand shapes needed

◆ Name ______________________________

Foot size

◆ Draw your foot shape in this box.

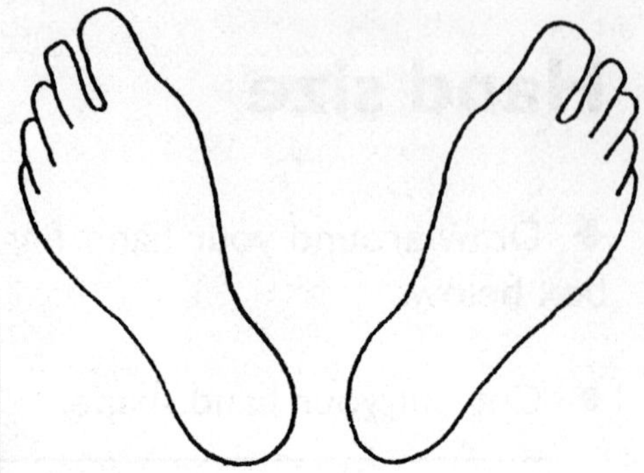

◆ How many cubes fit on your foot shape?

______________ cubes

◆ How many counters fit on your foot shape?

______________ counters

◆ Or bricks?

______________ bricks

◆ Find some other objects around the classroom that can be covered by the same number of cubes or counters as your foot shape. Write them here:

____

____

____

____

____

____

◆ How much bigger is your foot shape than your hand shape?

____

◆ Name ____________________

How many?

◆ How many triangles are there in each shape below? Write how many in the little boxes underneath.

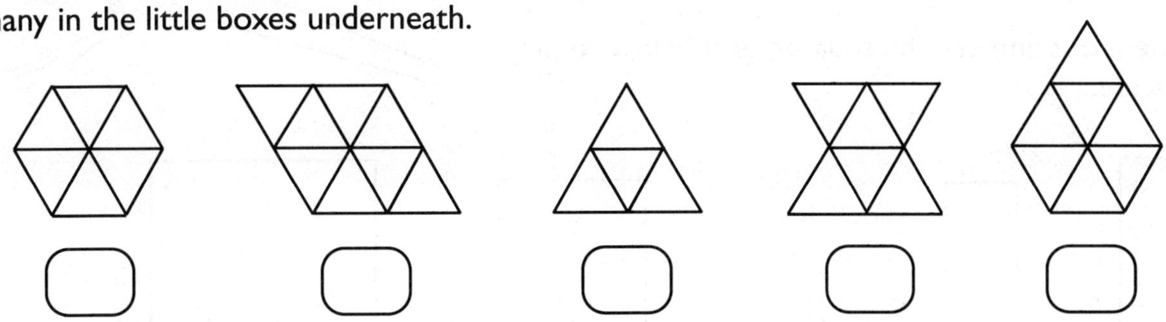

◆ How many rectangles are there in each of these shapes?

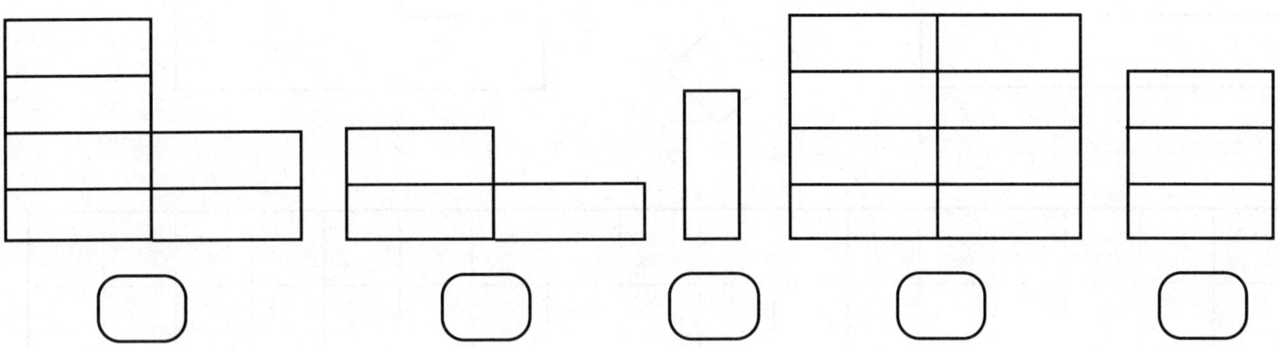

◆ How many squares are there in each of these shapes?

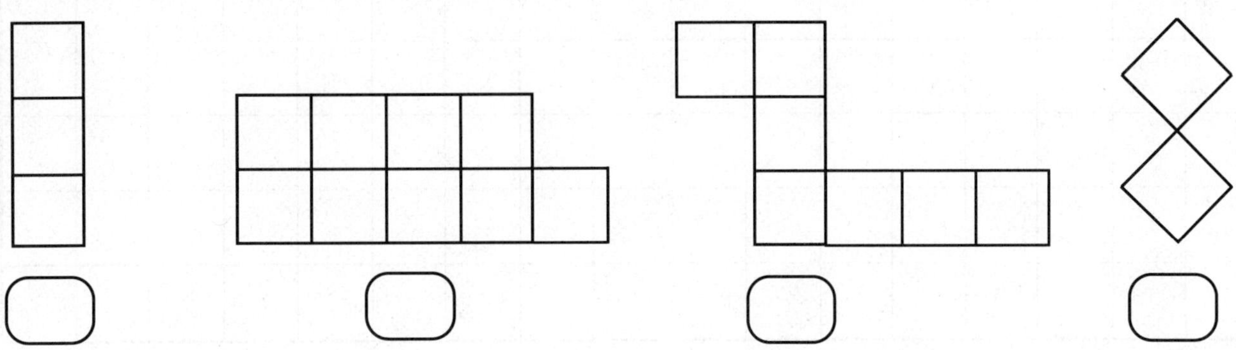

◆ Of all the shapes on the sheet:

- which has the largest area? ____________________
- which has the smallest area? ____________________

◆ How did you decide ? ____________________

____

◆ Name ______________________________

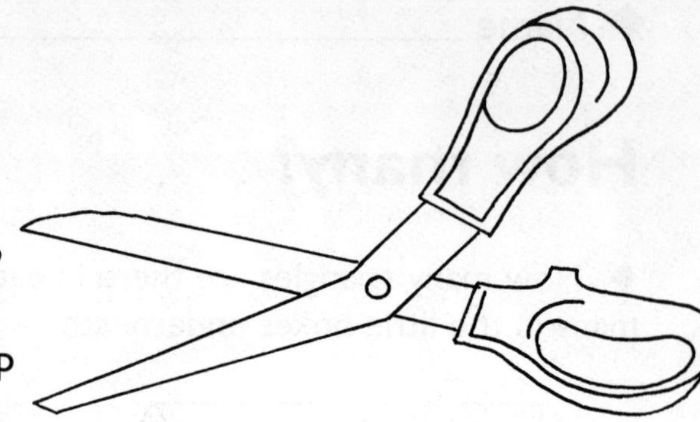

How many squares?

◆ How many squares does each of these shapes cover?

◆ Cut them out and use the squared grid below to help you to decide.

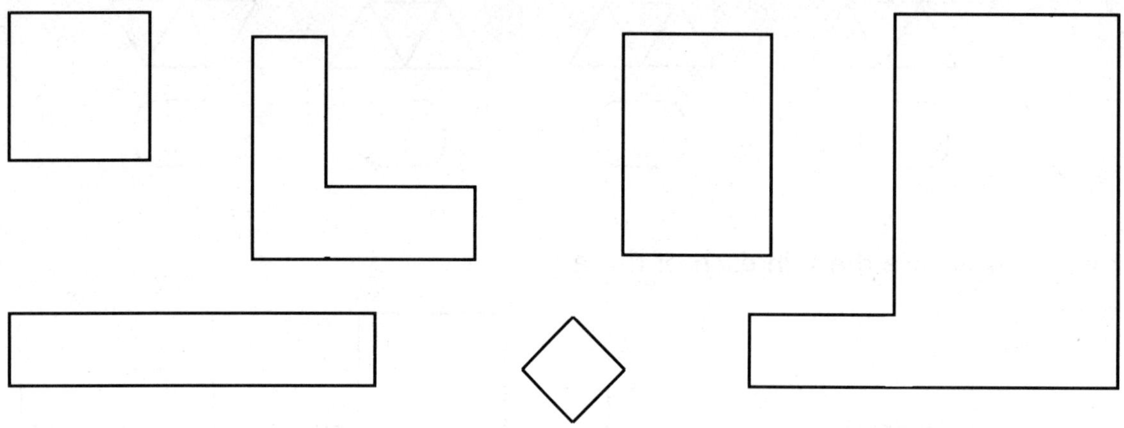

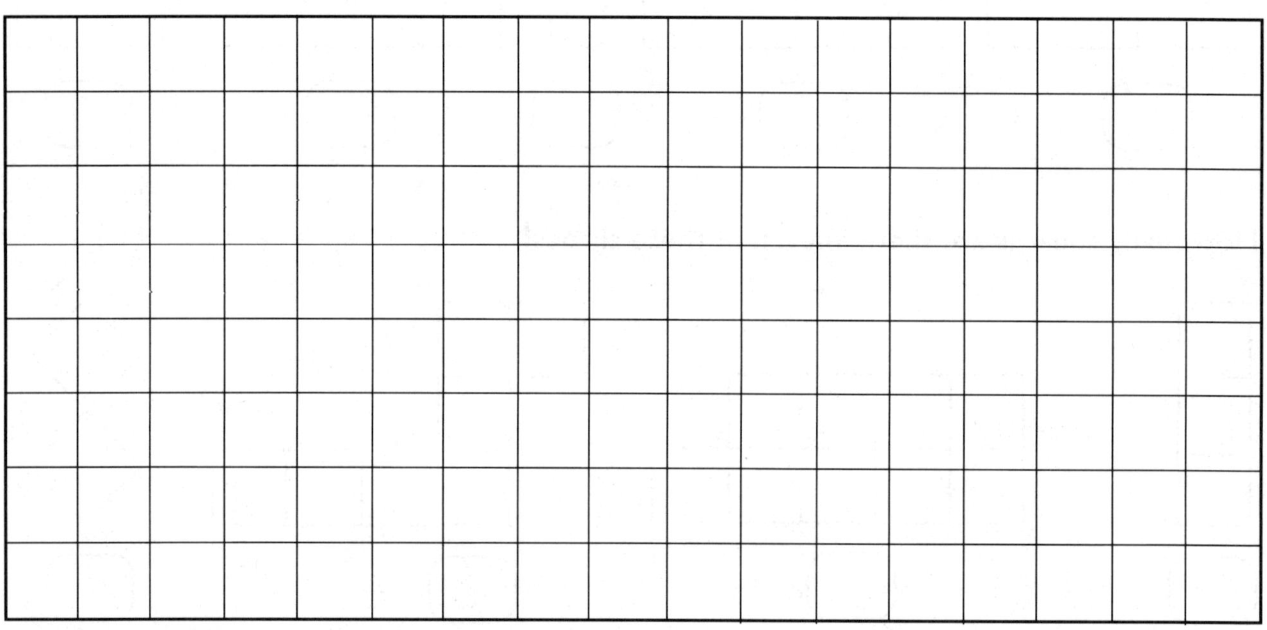

◆ Record your answers here:

Shape	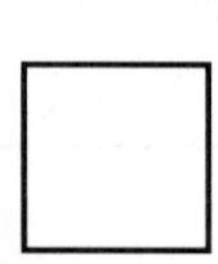	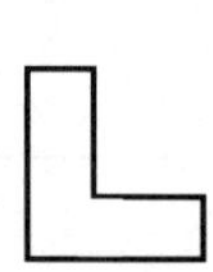		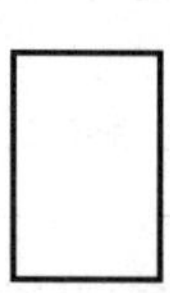	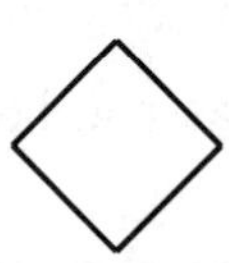	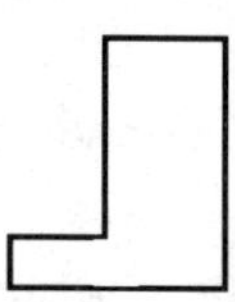
Number of squares covered						

◆ Name ______________________________

How many triangles?

Each of the shapes below covers an exact number of triangles.

◆ Cut them out and use the isometric paper below to help you to find out how many triangles they each cover.

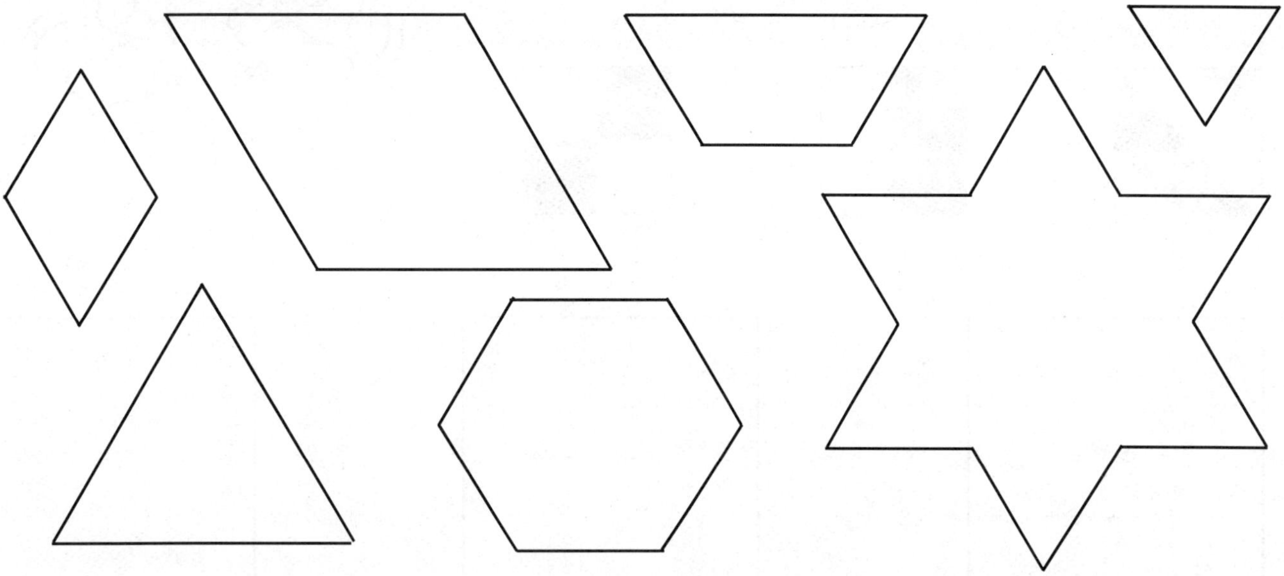

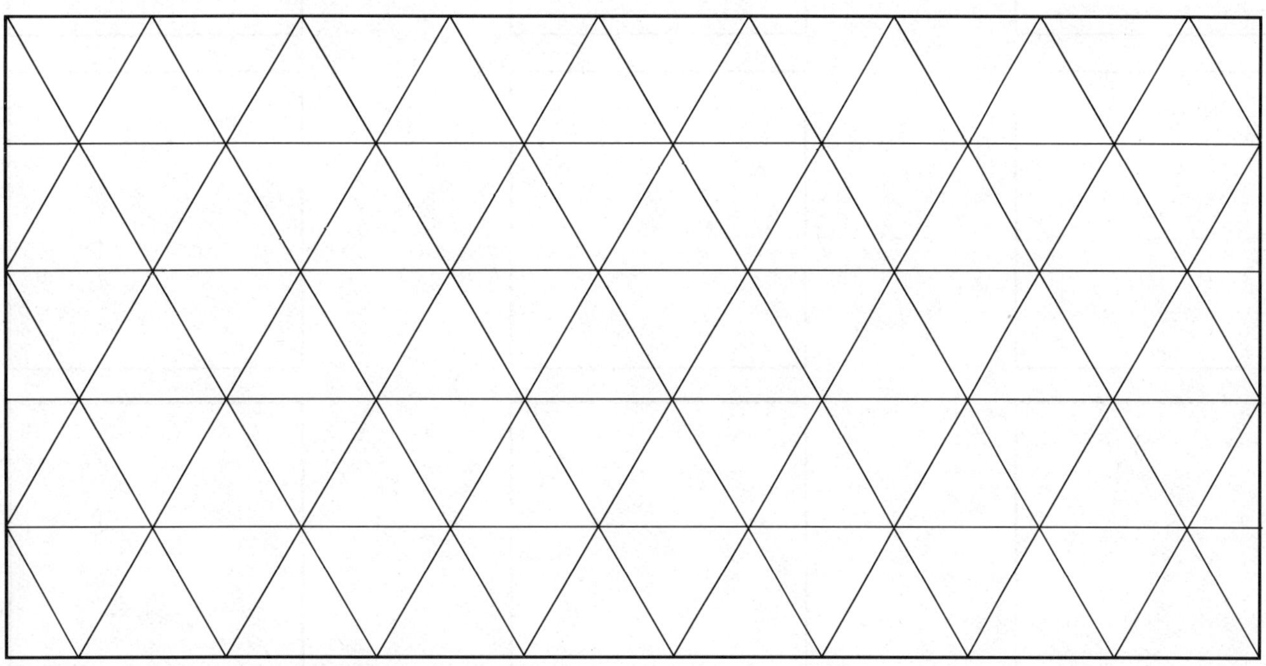

◆ Record your answers here:

Shape					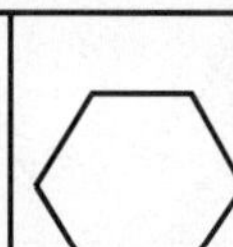		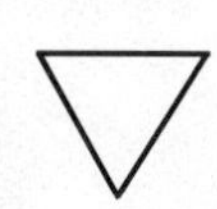
Number of triangles covered							

◆ Name ______________________________

Half a square

◆ Halve each of these squares.

Make sure each one is different, for example:

◆ Name ______________________

Counting the halves

◆ How many squares do these shapes cover? Remember that two half squares make one whole square.

◆ Write beside each shape how many squares they cover.

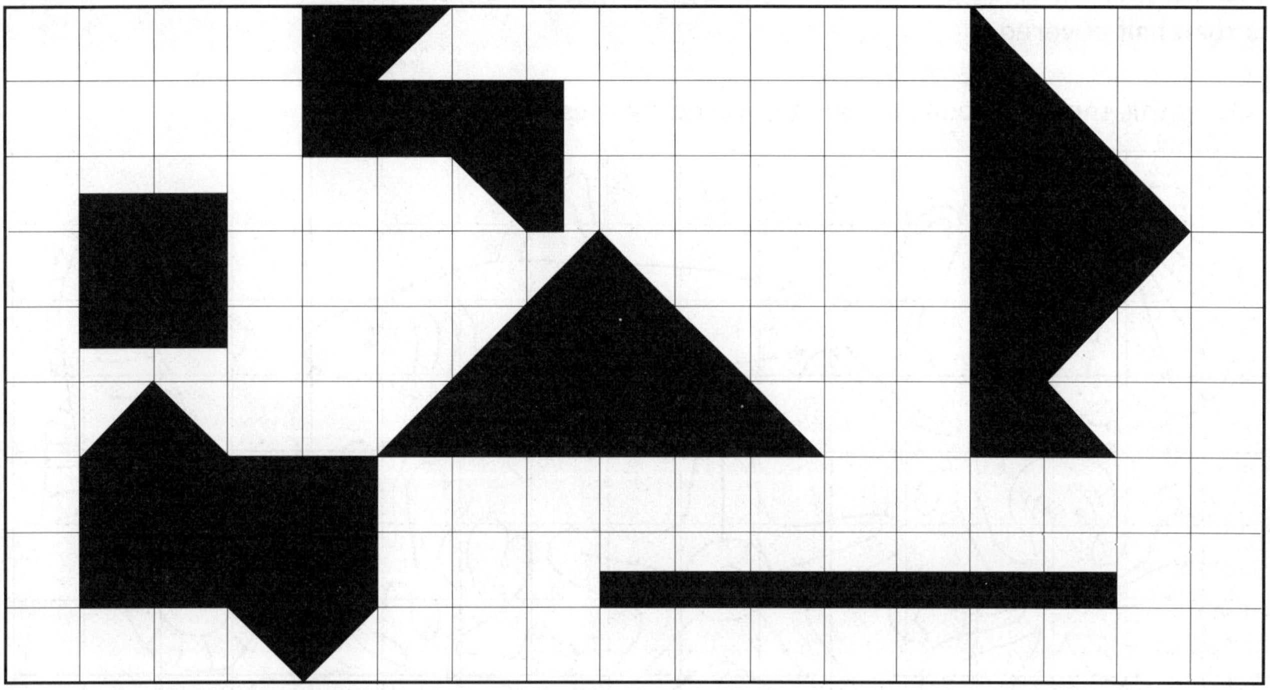

◆ Now choose an area, for example ten squares.

◆ Draw different shapes which cover this area. Use some half squares in each shape.

◆ Name ____________________

Counting curves

Usually, the areas you want to measure won't fit nicely into squares and half squares.

You can find an approximate area by **counting** any squares that are **more** than half covered as one square, and **ignoring** the ones that are **less** than half covered.

◆ Using this method, count the area covered by these shapes:

Picture	Number of squares	Picture	Number of squares
octopus		sea-horse	
shark		seaweed	
starfish		shell	

◆ Compare your answers with someone else.

◆ Are they the same? ____________________

◆ If not, why not? What do you think has happened? ____________________

____

____

____

◆ Name ______________________________

Making pairs

You will need: two copies of this sheet.

A

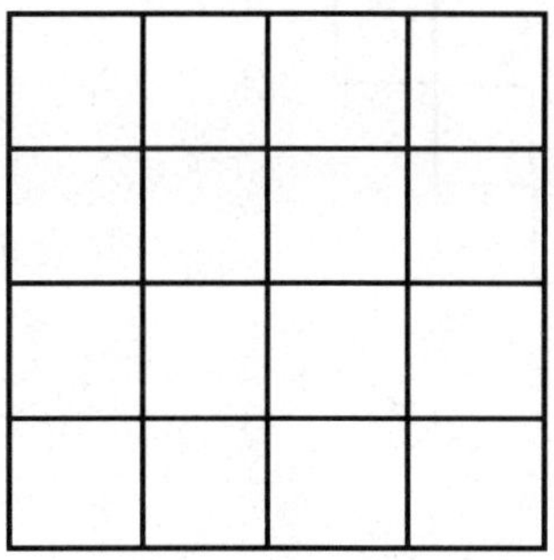

B

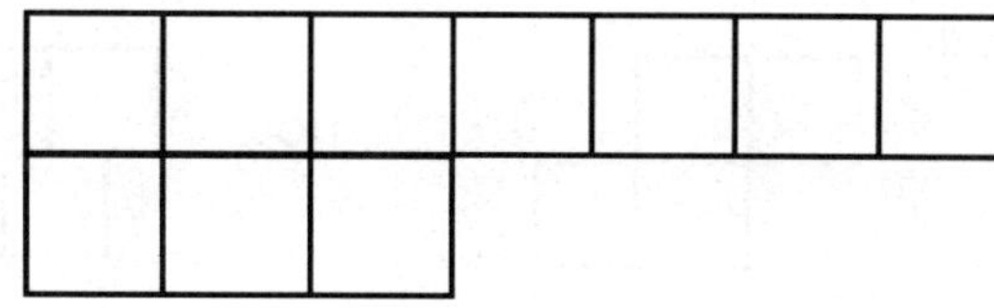

C

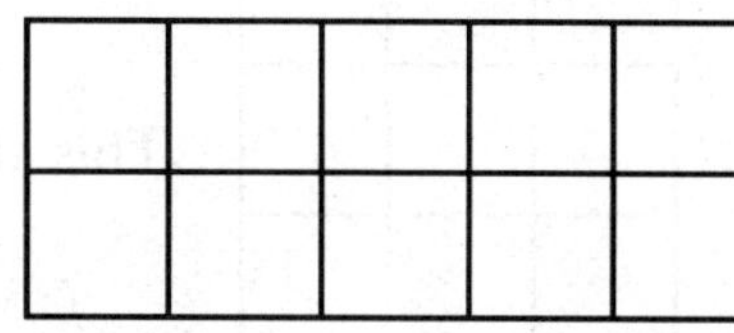

D

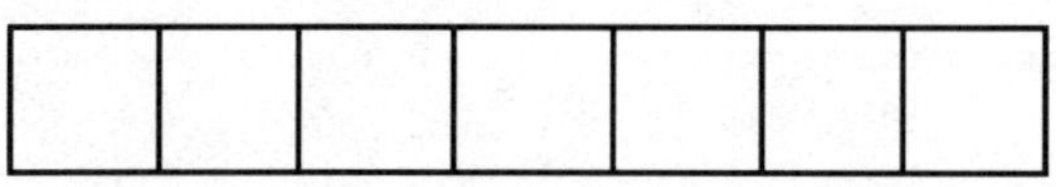

F

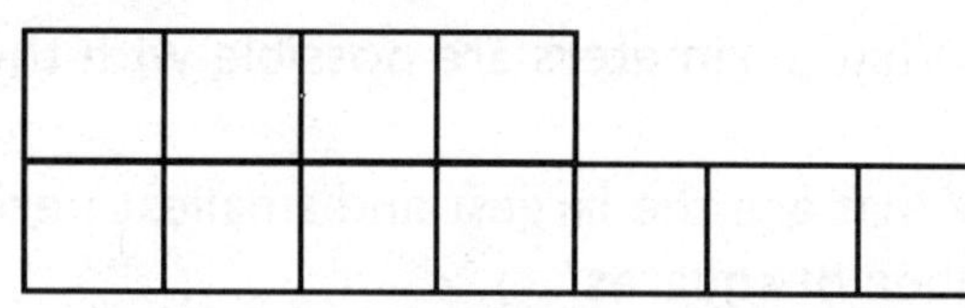

E

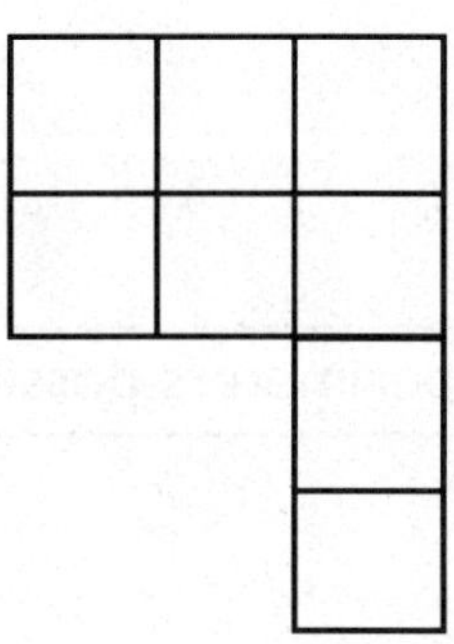

G

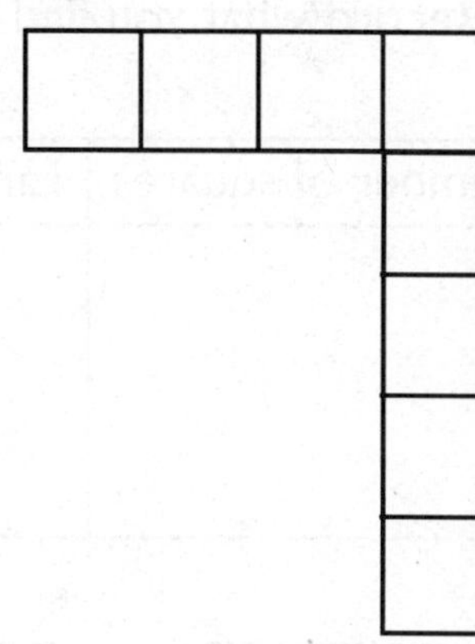

J

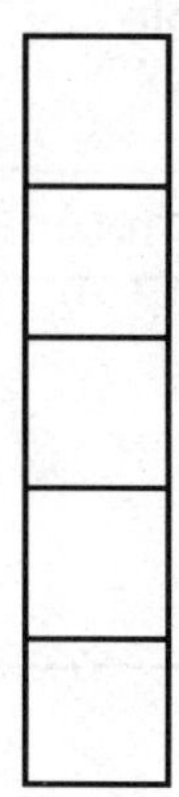

H

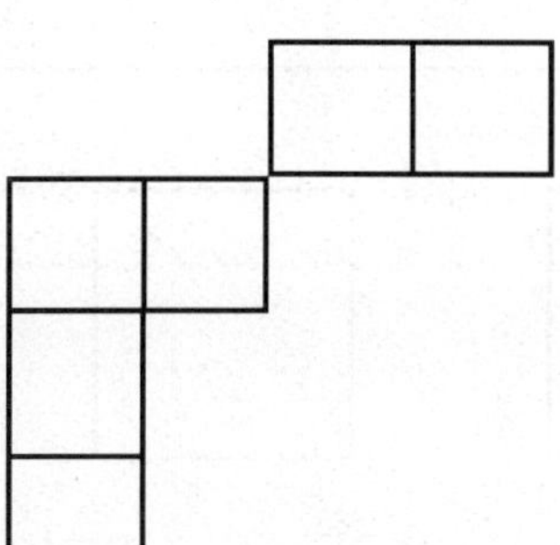

◆ Cut out the shapes on one sheet and pair them up according to the number of squares they contain.

◆ Cut out the shapes on the second sheet, and pair them up according to their perimeters.

◆ Make a display of your findings.

◆ Name ______________________

Arranging squares – 1

You are going to investigate arrangements of squares. The squares must touch along at least one edge, not just at the corners, and nor must they overlap.

That is: 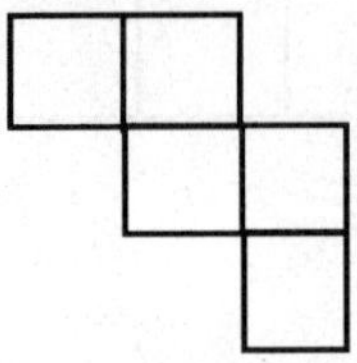 not: 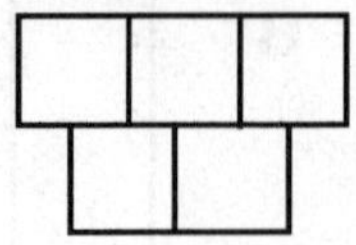 nor: 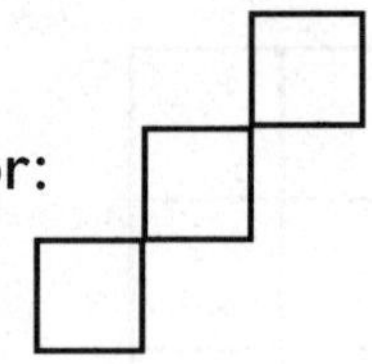

For each arrangement, count round to find the perimeter.

For example: 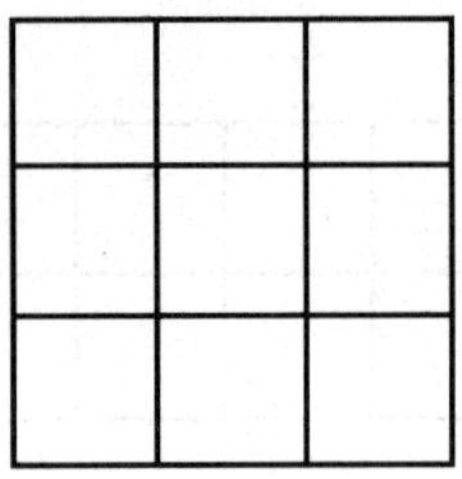 This shape has a perimeter of 12.

- ◆ Cut out the squares from the bottom of the page.
- ◆ Choose a number of squares from the ones you have cut out.
- ◆ What perimeters are possible with them?
- ◆ What are the largest and smallest perimeters you can find with this number of squares?
- ◆ Record what you find in this table.

Number of squares	Largest perimeter	Smallest perimeter	Other perimeters possible

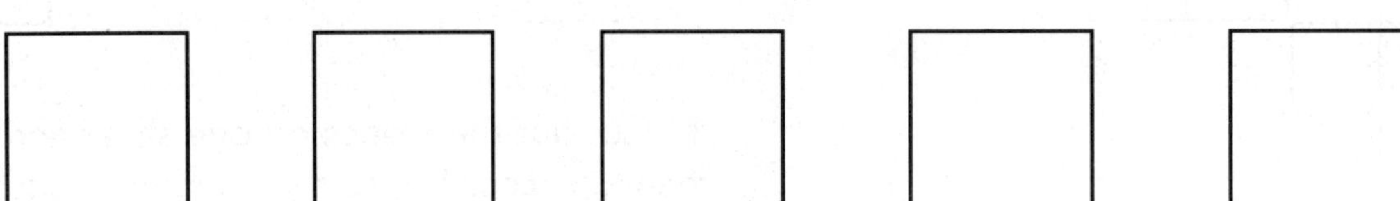

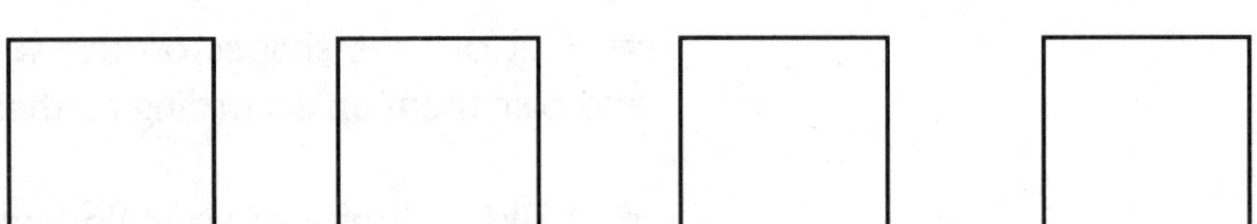

◆ Name ______________________________

Arranging squares – 2

Now you are going to investigate the perimeters that are possible for other numbers of your squares.

◆ For each number of squares, find out:
- the largest perimeter possible;
- the smallest perimeter possible;
- what other perimeters can be made.

◆ Record your findings, for each number of squares, in the table.

Number of squares	Largest perimeter	Smallest perimeter	Other perimeters possible

Write here about anything interesting that you noticed, for example patterns, surprises or puzzles.

◆ Name ______________________________

Perimeter possibilities – 1

What different areas can be enclosed when the perimeter is 18cm?

◆ Draw as many such areas as you can on the squared grid below.

◆ Compare your shapes with those made by other people.

◆ How many different shapes have you found between you? ______________________

◆ Cut them out and make a display.

◆ Name ______________________________

Perimeter possibilities – 2

◆ If the perimeter must still be 18cm, what different areas can be enclosed on the isometric grid below?

Notice that the side of each small triangle is 2cm.

◆ How many different shapes have you made?

____

◆ Use some more squared and isometric paper. Choose another perimeter and explore the different areas that are possible.

◆ Name ______________________ and ______________________

Rectangles – 1

◆ Work with a partner.

◆ On the squared grid below, draw as many different rectangles as you can that cover 24 squares. You may need some more squared paper.

◆ Label each rectangle with a letter.

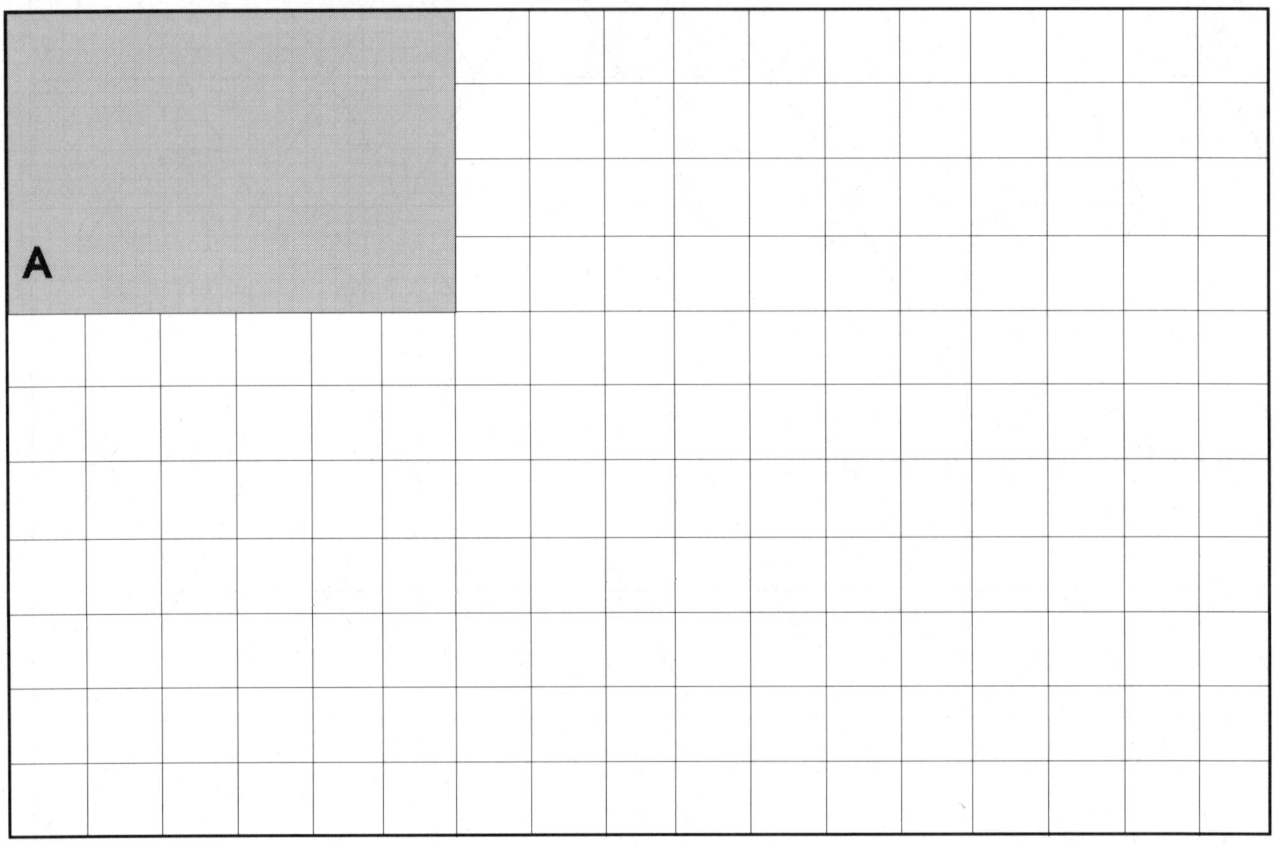

◆ Write down the sizes of your rectangles on the table below. One has been done for you.

Rectangle	Across	Down	Rectangle	Across	Down
A	6	4			

◆ Name ______________________ and ______________________

Rectangles – 2

◆ Choose another number of squares, for example 16.

◆ Investigate how many rectangles you can make with them.

◆ Record your rectangles here.

Rectangle	Across	Down	Rectangle	Across	Down

◆ Choose other numbers of squares and investigate how many rectangles can be made from each. You will need more squared paper for this.

◆ Be ready to talk about:

- which number of squares produced the most rectangles;
- which numbers of squares produced very few rectangles;
- anything else you have discovered.

◆ Name ____________________

How many hidden squares?

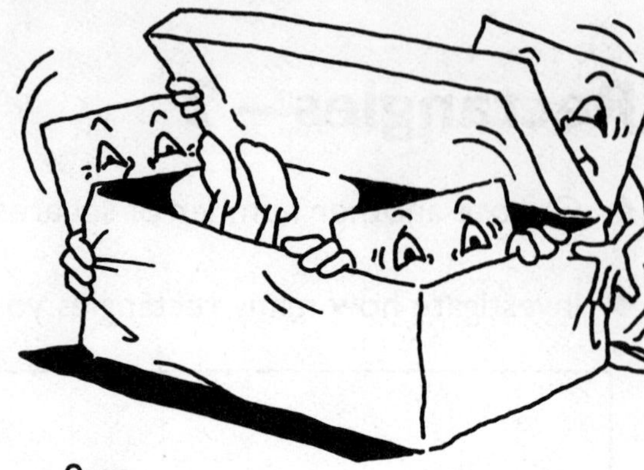

◆ The sizes of these rectangles are marked.
How many square centimetres do they cover?

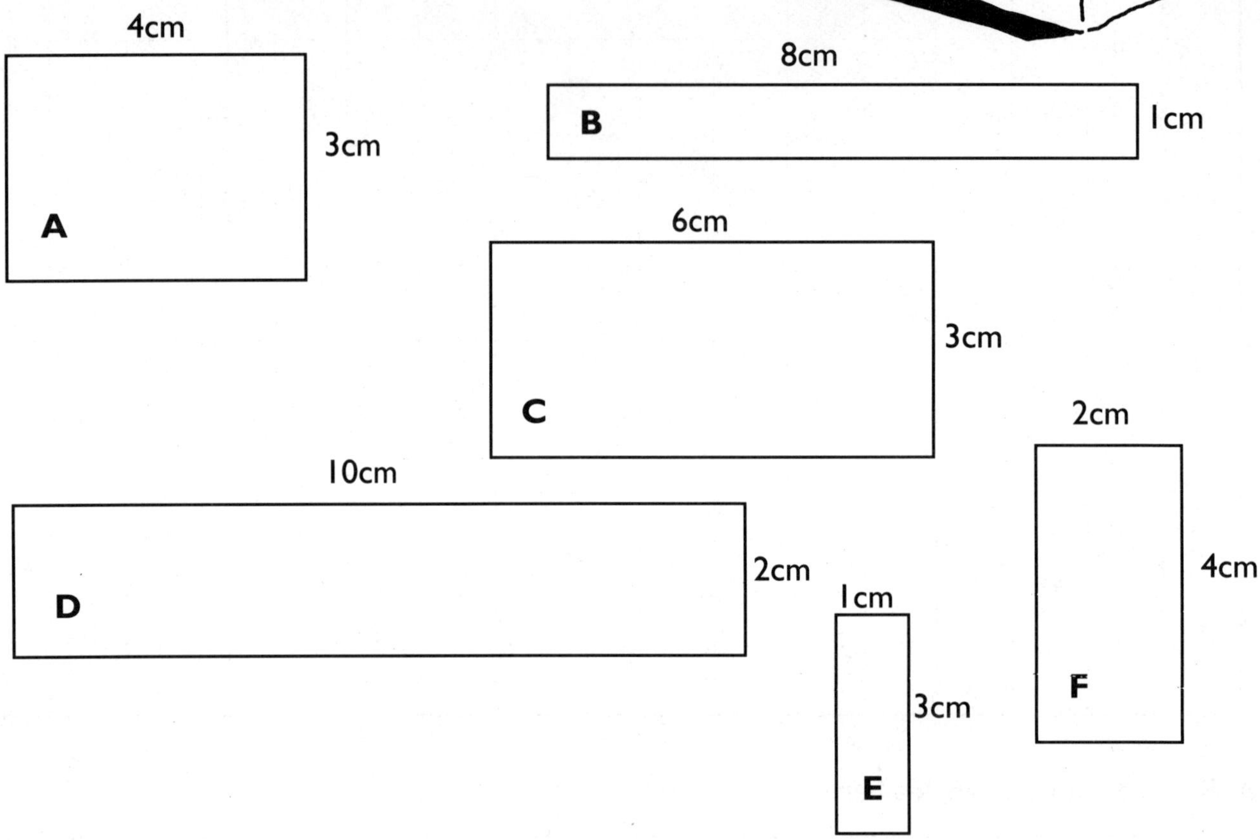

◆ Record your answers on this chart.

A	sq. cms	**D**	
B		**E**	
C		**F**	

◆ Explain here how you worked out the answers. ____________________

____

____

◆ Draw some more rectangles on plain paper
and ask someone else to work out the hidden squares.

◆ Name ______________________________

Tangram

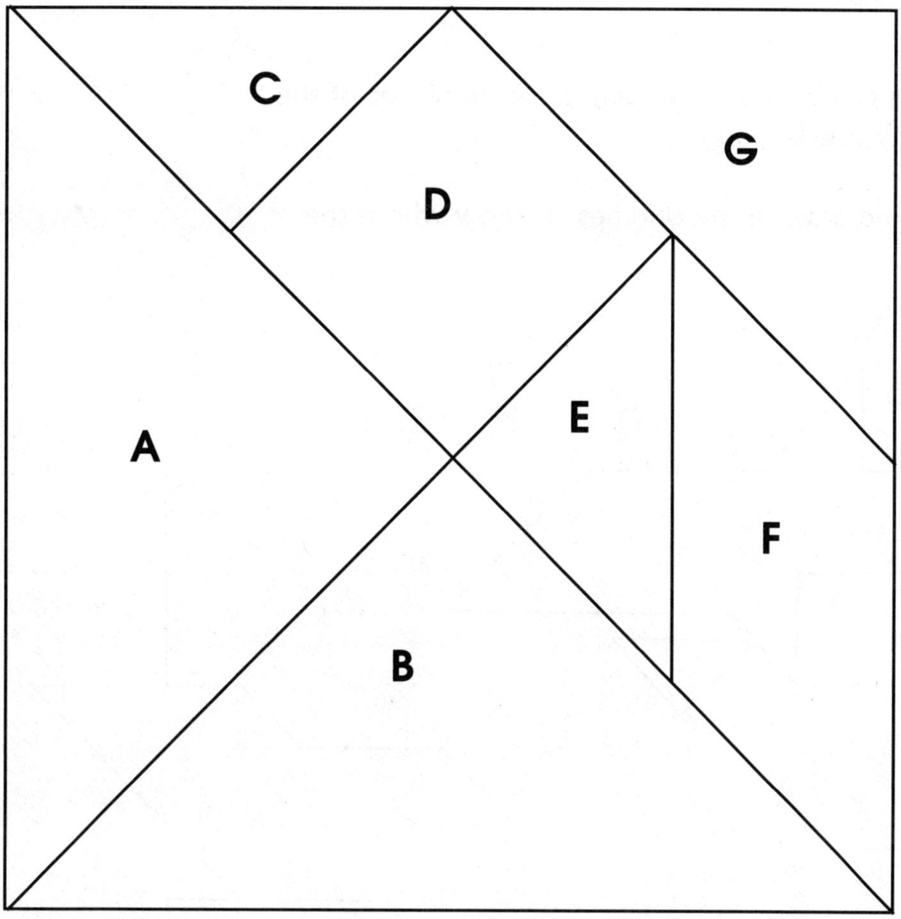

This Chinese puzzle is called a 'tangram'.
The size of each piece has been specially chosen.

◆ Cut out the tangram and find out how the pieces match up.
Two pieces together could match another, for instance.

Record your findings here.

◆ Name ______________________

Tangram puzzles

Each of these shapes can be made by using all seven pieces of the tangram (without any overlapping).

◆ Make each one and draw in the outlines to show where the pieces fit.

◆ Arrange the pieces into other shapes. Draw round the outlines on to plain paper and then offer them to someone else to solve.

◆ Name ______________________________

Tangram illusions

Two mathematicians, called Sam Loyd and H.E. Dudeney, loved tangrams. Below are some puzzling combinations they discovered.

◆ Arrange your seven tangram pieces to match these outlines and then mark in where the pieces fit.

The black sections are spaces!

◆ What is rather strange about them?

◆ Name ______________________

Framing miniatures – I

The drawings of these miniatures show their actual sizes. Glass and wood are needed to make frames for these miniatures.

◆ Work out how much wood and glass will be needed for each frame, and record the amounts in the chart below. You can cut out the pictures if this helps.

Picture	Size of glass	Length of wood to make frame
Grandma	sq. cms	cm
The twins		
The dog		
Mum and the baby		

◆ Name ______________________________

Framing miniatures – 2

◆ If glass costs 3p for one square centimetre and framing costs 3p per centimetre, how much will framing each picture cost?

Picture	Cost of glass	Cost of frame	Total

You can use this space to do any working out.

◆ Use squared paper to investigate whether it is possible to have framed pictures where:

- the glass costs exactly twice as much as the frame;
- the glass costs the same as the frame.

◆ Write here what you find out. ______________________________

◆ Name ______________________________

A farmer and his field

A farmer has 36 identical fence panels, with which he wants to build a sheep pen.

The bigger the space he can enclose with them, the more pleased he will be.

◆ Explore the different shapes and sizes of field he can enclose. (Squared, triangular or spotty paper may help you.)

◆ Draw or describe some of your suggested shapes of sheep pen here and explain why the farmer might choose one.

2cm squared paper

I cm squared paper

Triangular (isometric) paper

Spotty paper (squared and triangular)

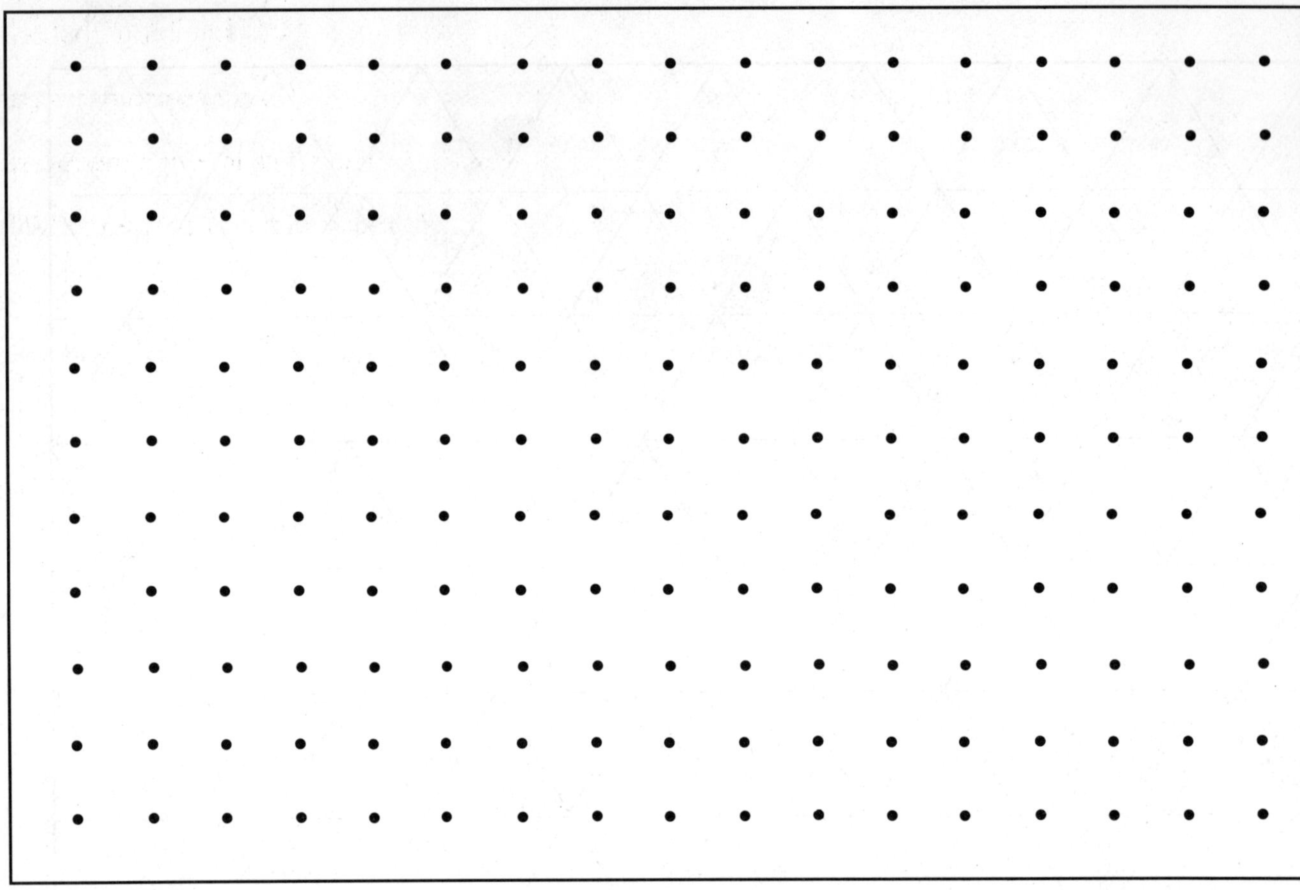

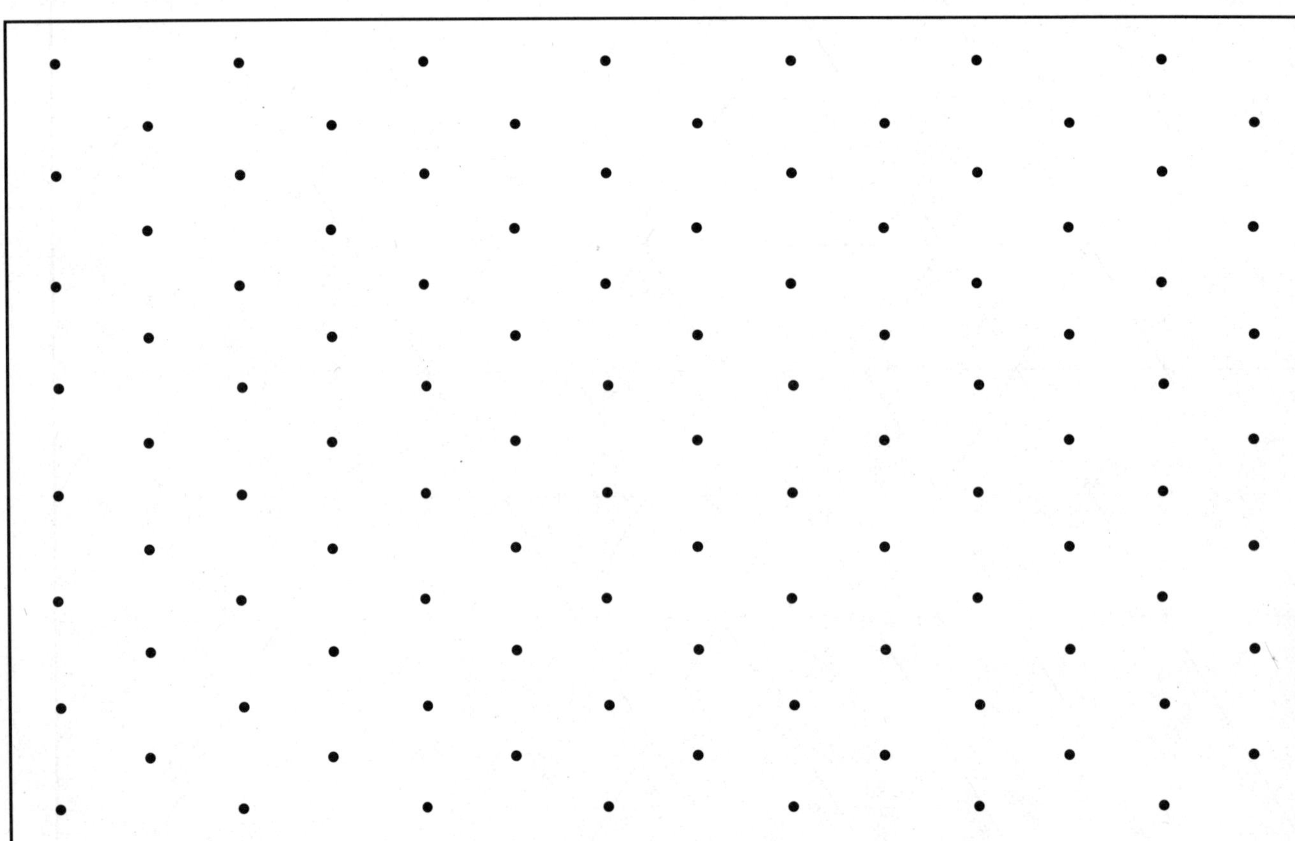